PLANTING THE SEEDS

A Curriculum for HBCU Awareness

Phyllis M. Wilson, Ph.D
Lead Developer

Arnater M. Dowers and Carol Hedgepeth
Contributors and Co-Presenters

authorHOUSE®

AuthorHouse™
1663 Liberty Drive
Bloomington, IN 47403
www.authorhouse.com
Phone: 833-262-8899

Published by AuthorHouse 08/26/2021

ISBN: 978-1-6655-3647-9 (sc)
ISBN: 978-1-6655-3646-2 (e)

Library of Congress Control Number: 2021917534

CONTENTS

ACKNOWLEDGEMENT

I want to express my sincere appreciation to my two Contributors and Co-Presenters-Arnater M. Dowers and Carol Hedgepeth. You gave your all to ensure that the program was successful. Love you both.

Dr. Sandra Thomas, Dr. LaQuita Carter, and, Dr. Natalie Coleman. You are the best examples I know of role models for every African American student you come into contact with. So proud to have had the opportunity to be in your lives. Your success is never ending with more to come.

INTRODUCTION

Planting The Seeds was a program specifically designed to expose more minority students to the existence and opportunities provided by attending one of the more than 140 Historically Black colleges and Universities. A partnership that was developed between two organizations, allowed the individuals involved in the creation and implementation of the program to expose a group of middle school students to the program. While the original audience were in grades 6-8, students in grades 9 and 10 can also be provided the program content. The enthusiasm and knowledge that were displayed by the participants throughout the delivery of the program content reinforced the importance of exposing more minority students to this valuable program content. The more the information was shared, the more those of us who had not attended an HBCU, wish that we had done so.

Although the program was provided over a number of months, there is great flexibility to adjust the time frame for presenting the Planting The Seeds program. The content can be shared on a daily basis, a weekly basis, or a monthly basis depending on the students being served and their schedules. Although the schedules may be changed and require adaptability, the content remains relevant and consistent. We say to all those who implement the curriculum that is shared, you will make a difference in the life of every student who participate in the program. The goal to attend college will now be combined with the selection of a Historically Black College or University. And life will be all the better for doing so.

Planting the Seeds

Knowledge · Inspiration · Goal Setting · Action Steps

PHYLLIS M. WILSON, PH.D

PROGRAM DESCRIPTION

A broad range of activities and events were provided specifically intended to increase the awareness of existing HBCU's and their offerings. A tree symbol that showed the names of all existing HBCU's was created. The names, locations and more detailed coverage of the locations, majors, rankings, etc. were discussed over the duration of the sessions. The students were given the opportunity to express their potential career choices, wishes and future plans, SMART Goals were defined and developed by each student in order to align their future plans, career possibilities, and the HBCU's that would best support their successful achievement.

Students were asked to sign the program participation commitment form developed specifically for the HBCU exploration. The expectation of full attendance and involvement on a monthly basis were included in the participation agreement. The monthly program identified students as members of The Genius Club with an accompanying pledge stated at the beginning of each session. A copy of the pledge was given to each student for use beyond the sessions. The pledge was intended to encourage students to believe in themselves; and, be a reminder that they had the capability to achieve at the highest levels as they strived to succeed in their life mission. An in service for parents was conducted by those leading the program. The overview of the program content and intent were shared with parents in order to garner support for the program.

Activities engaged in during the conduct of the program included creating a list of the 5 things looked for in a college students would like to attend. This list was used to measure the compatibility with some of the listed HBCU's. Students were guided through the activity of doing computer research to see what opportunities could be gained from enrolling at the HBCU's they had placed on their lists. A Guest Speaker, Dr. Ravi Jitta addressed the students and described his career choice and college preparation steps.

One of the culminating events occurred in January when a college fair featuring 3 Florida universities (Edward Water, Florida Memorial, Bethune Cookman) and their representatives was held. This event allowed students the opportunity to hear extensive amount of information about the colleges in a face-to-face setting with the representatives. Another area covered in the sessions was the comprehensive coverage of STEM (Science, Technology, Engineering and Math) careers and the career options available in these areas. African Americans who had succeeded in these fields were highlighted in one of the sessions. Much discussion occurred throughout the sessions about the career choices students were considering. The highlight of STEM careers was used to both expand student knowledge and to include the consideration in their futures. Students were requested to identify their career choices and narrow down the list of HBCU's that best aligned with those choices. Students in the program planned to be lawyers, doctors (pediatrician) and in the health care field (nurses).

The final session recognized those students who had actively participated in the program with certificates and small gifts distributed. A video was made of student sharing what they valued most from the sessions.

PRESENTATION COMPONENTS FOR POTENTIAL PARTNERS

1. Share who we are.

2. Share the project intent.

3. Share the project content.

4. Share project time frame.

5. Respond to any questions.

6. Solicit suggestions and recommendations that will enhance partnership.

7. Share the Memorandum of Understanding and Program Participation Agreement.

8. Identify next steps.

MEMORANDUM OF UNDERSTANDING

The partnership will be based on the National organization focus on expanding enrollment at Historically Black Colleges and Universities (HBCUs). The partnership program offered is called "Planting the Seed" and will be focused on providing mentoring for participating students and an overview of HBCU's.

The project goals include:

1. Providing knowledge to students about the existence and services available at HBCU's.
2. Inspiring students to pursue attendance at an HBCU.
3. Motivating each student to develop specific goals focused on acquiring the grade point average and other specific skills necessary for acceptance at an HBCU.
4. Implementing, by students, a specific set of actions and strategies designed to accomplish all goals that have been set.
5. Incorporating into the mentoring component of the Planting the Seeds program. Activities that will occur on a monthly basis beginning in September 2016 and ending in June 2017, unless date modifications are agreed upon by both partners.

PHYLLIS M. WILSON, PH.D

Each participating partner will cooperate fully and communicate regularly to ensure that students benefit fully from the services provided. The expected program outcomes are:

1. Students will have the fullest amount of information needed to make the best college selection decision possible.
2. Parents will play an active role in the college selection process.
3. The creation of a strong cooperative and collaborative project so that students are positively impacted.

PLANTING THE SEEDS
MENTOR TRAINING

September 24, 2016

The key components for the mentor /student interaction are as follows:

1. Building a connection with students by having meaningful conversations.

    A. Focus on students' opinions
    B. Identify the students' concerns, questions, and needs based on what is shared by the students with you.
    C. Ask clarifying questions.
    D. Emphasize your willingness to be there for the student to support their efforts.
    E. Adapt your conversational style to the expressed information from the students and what the current situation requires.
    F. Be the best possible listener you can be.

2. Role model for students the kind of behavior and treatment you want to see them display.

    A. Be as respectful as possible throughput interactions with students. By doing so, you are able to expect the same from them.
    B. Share with students the kind of behaviors displayed by successful people so that they can begin to Incorporate these behaviors into their repertoire.

3. Show the students on a regular basis that you genuinely care about them and the future that lies ahead of them.

    A. Students need to know that you recognize their humanness and wish to make a contribution to both their present and their future
    B. Treat them with the kindness they deserve.
    C. Be fully present in every way that you can. Know that you are important to their lives.

PROGRAM PARTICIPATION COMMITMENT

Mentor: As a mentor, I commit to:

1. Providing participants with sufficient information to make informed and knowledgeable decisions.
2. Being available at time and dates I have agreed upon.
3. Providing the necessary support assistance and advocacy that will best meet the needs of participants.
4. Serving as role model for program.

Student: As a participant I commit to:

1. Completing all actions and activities as appropriate requested of me.
2. Pursue finding answer to any and all question I may have regarding Historically Black Colleges and Universities.
3. Focusing on obtaining the needed assistance that will contribute to improvements in my grade point average.
4. Demonstrating support for other students in as many ways as I can.

5. Showing respect and consideration for all those connected with the program as well as others in my environment.

Mentor Signature:_____ Date:_____

Student Signature:_____ Date: _____

National Historically Black colleges and Universities Initiatives

Program: "Planting the Seeds"
(Proposal April 16, 2016)

Introduction

Presented by:

Dr. Phyllis Wilson

Origin of HBCU National Initiative

President Barack Obama

In a presidential proclamation observing 2011 HBCU Week, President Obama remarked:

HBCUs continue a proud tradition as vibrant centers of intellectual inquiry and engines of scientific discovery and innovation. New waves of students, faculty, and alumni are building on their rich legacies and helping America achieve our goal of once again leading the world in having the highest proportion of college graduates by 2020.

U.S. Department of Education, (2016, March 22). *White House Initiative on Historica*'*ly Black Colleges and Universities.* Retrieved from URL

Purpose:

- ▲ To inform students and their parents about the existence and value of Historically Black Colleges and Universities.

- ▲ To engage students in the college application decision making process so that HBCU's receive full consideration.

- ▲ To serve as a knowledge source for those involved with students at the critical decision making time frame.

- ▲ To provide mentoring and tutoring services for identified student groups.

Mission:

- "Contribute to the formulation of a positive, productive, and culturally diverse society". The mission of "Planting the Seed" program is to provide a high level of information about availability and benefits of attending an HBCU. Students will become inspired to establish the goal of selecting and applying at one or more of the HBCU's. Such consideration will add to the diversity of options and choices.

Vision:

► Our vision is for all students participating in the "Planting the Seeds" program to pursue enrollment at one of the Historically Black Colleges and Universities.

Goals:

▲ 1. To provide sufficient knowledge for full consideration of attendance at HBCU's.

▲ 2. To inspire students based on the information and encouragement provided to include applications to HBCU's as part of their college application process.

▲ 3. To assist students to establish relevant academic and personal goals that will aid in their acceptance at a Historically Black College and University.

▲ 4. To utilize the goals that have been developed to create a specific set of action steps, that each student will take to best ensure admission to the selected HBCU.

Mentor Role for HBCU Initiative Program

▲ Inform

▲ Assist

▲ Support

▲ Advocate

Historically Black Colleges
and
Universities

Presented by:
Arnater M. Dowers

Background Information

- A. Definition of HBCU's

- B. List and Location of HBCU's

Definition of HBCU's INNOVATORS FOR FUTURE SUCCESS

▶ The Higher Education Act of 1965, as amended, defines an HBCU as :
"....any historically black college or university that was established prior to 1964, whose principal mission was, and is, the education of black Americans, and that is accredited by a nationally recognized accrediting agency or association determined by the Secretary [of Education] to be reliable authority as to the quality of training offered or is, according to such an agency or association, making reasonable progress toward accreditation." HBCUs offer all students, regardless of race, an opportunity to develop their skills and talents. These Institutions train young people who go on to serve domestically and internationally in the professions as entrepreneurs and in the public and private sectors. HBCUs are a source of accomplishment and great pride for the African American community as well as the entire nation

U.S. Department of Education, (2016, March 22). *What are HBCUs?* Retrieved from URL

SCHOOL	CITY	STATE
A&M University	Huntsville	Alabama
Alabama State University	Montgomery	Alabama
Albany State University	Albany	Georgia
Alcorn State University	Lorman	Mississippi
Allen University	Columbia	South Carolina
American Baptist College	Nashville	Tennessee
University of Arkansas at Pine Bluff	Pine Bluff	Arkansas
Arkansas Baptist College	Little Rock	Arkansas
Barber-Scotia College	Concord	North Carolina
Benedict College	Columbia	South Carolina
Bennett College	Greensboro	North Carolina
Bethune-Cookman University	Daytona Beach	Florida
Bishop State Community College	Mobile	Alabama
Bluefield State College	Bluefield	West Virginia
Bowie State University	Bowie	Maryland
Central State University	Wilberforce	Ohio
Cheyney University of Pennsylvania	Cheyney	Pennsylvania
Claflin University	Orangeburg	South Carolina
Clark Atlanta University	Atlanta	Georgia
Clinton Junior College	Rock Hill	South Carolina
Coahoma Community College	Coahoma County	Mississippi
Concordia College, Alabama	Selma	Alabama
Coppin State University	Baltimore	Maryland

SCHOOL	CITY	STATE
Delaware State University	Dover	Delaware
Denmark Technical College	Denmark	South Carolina
Dillard University	New Orleans	Louisiana
University of the District of Columbia	Washington	District of Columbia
Edward Waters College	Jacksonville	Florida
Elizabeth City State University	Elizabeth City	North Carolina
Fayetteville State University	Fayetteville	North Carolina
Fisk University	Nashville	Tennessee
Florida A&M University	Tallahassee	Florida
Florida Memorial University	Miami Gardens	Florida
Fort Valley State University	Fort Valley	Georgia
Gadsden State Community College	Gadsden	Alabama
Grambling State University	Grambling	Louisiana
Hampton University	Hampton	Virginia
Harris-Stowe State University	St. Louis	Missouri
Hinds Community College at Utica	Utica	Mississippi
Howard University	Washington	District of Columbia
Huston-Tillotson University	Austin	Texas
Interdenominational Theological Center	Atlanta	Georgia
J. F. Drake State Technical College	Huntsville	Alabama
Jackson State University	Jackson	Mississippi
Jarvis Christian College	Hawkins	Texas
Johnson C. Smith University	Charlotte	North Carolina

SCHOOL	CITY	STATE
Kentucky State University	Frankfort	Kentucky
Knoxville College	Knoxville (Mechanicsville)	Tennessee
Lane College	Jackson	Tennessee
Langston University	Langston	Oklahoma
Lawson State Community College	Bessemer	Alabama
LeMoyne-Owen College	Memphis	Tennessee
Lincoln University	Chester County	Pennsylvania
Lincoln University of Missouri	Jefferson City	Missouri
Livingstone College	Salisbury	North Carolina
University of Maryland Eastern Shore	Princess Anne	Maryland
Meharry Medical College	Nashville	Tennessee
Miles College	Fairfield	Alabama
Mississippi Valley State University	Itta Bena	Mississippi
Morehouse College	Atlanta	Georgia
Morehouse School of Medicine	Atlanta	Georgia
Morgan State University	Baltimore	Maryland
Morris Brown College	Atlanta	Georgia
Morris College	Sumter	South Carolina
Norfolk State University	Norfolk	Virginia
North Carolina Agricultural & Technical State University	Greensboro	North Carolina
North Carolina Central University	Durham	North Carolina
Oakwood University	Huntsville	Alabama
Paine College	Augusta	Georgia
Paul Quinn College	Dallas	Texas
Philander Smith College	Little Rock	Arkansas

SCHOOL	CITY	STATE
Prairie View A&M University	Prairie View	Texas
Rust College	Holly Springs	Mississippi
Savannah State University	Savannah	Georgia
Selma University	Selma	Alabama
Shaw University	Raleigh	North Carolina
Shorter College	Little Rock	Arkansas
Shelton State Community College	Tuscaloosa	Alabama
Simmons College	Louisville	Kentucky
South Carolina State University	Orangeburg	South Carolina
Southern University at New Orleans	New Orleans	Louisiana
Southern University at Shreveport	Shreveport	Louisiana
Southern University and A&M College	Baton Rouge	Louisiana
Southwestern Christian College	Terrell	Texas
Spelman College	Atlanta	Georgia
St. Augustine's University	Raleigh	North Carolina
St. Philip's College	San Antonio	Texas
Stillman College	Tuscaloosa	Alabama
Talladega College	Talladega County	Alabama
Tennessee State University	Nashville	Tennessee
Texas College	Tyler	Texas
Texas Southern University	Houston	Texas
Tougaloo College	Hinds County	Mississippi
Trenholm State Technical College	Montgomery	Alabama
Tuskegee University	Tuskegee	Alabama
University of the Virgin Islands	St. Croix & St. Thomas	United States Virgin Islands

SCHOOL	CITY	STATE	
Virginia State University	Petersburg	Virginia	
Virginia Union University	Richmond	Virginia	
Virginia University of Lynchburg	Lynchburg	Virginia	
Voorhees College	Denmark	South Carolina	
West Virginia State University	Institute	West Virginia	
Wilberforce University	Wilberforce	Ohio	
Wiley College	Marshall	Texas	
Winston-Salem State University	Winston-Salem	North Carolina	
Xavier University of Louisiana	New Orleans	Louisiana	

Niche (2014), *List of HBCUs by States*. Retrieved from URL

Top Ten HBCUs

Based on Niche's Best Colleges, this grade takes into account key factors such as the strength of the academic program, the aptitude of professors, the quality of campus amenities, the general character of student life, as well as student reviews in an attempt to measure the overall excellence of the college experience.

- Spelman College

- Howard University

- North Carolina A&T State University

- Xavier University of Louisiana

- Florida A&M University

- Tuskegee University

- Hampton University

- Tougaloo College

- Winston-Salman State University

- Prairie View A&M University

Niche, (2016).*Best HBCU Schools Ranking Methodology*. Retrieved form URL

Florida HBCUs

Florida Agriculture and Mechanical University (Tallahassee) (102 majors)

Bethune Cookman University (Daytona Beach) (37 majors)

Florida Memorial University (Miami Gardens) (34 majors)

Edward Waters College (Jacksonville) (15 majors)

HBCU College, (2016) *HBCU Schools in Florida*. Retrieved URL

Reasons to choose an HBCU

- A first - rate Education

- Caring professors and faculty

- Classes and extracurricular activities tailored to African Americans

- A supportive Atmosphere

- Diversity

- Empowerment

- A chance to continue the legacy

- Alumni associations for graduates of all HBCUs

- Scholarships and grants

- You'll be in Good Company

College Express (2016), *10 Reasons to Consider Going to an HBCU*. Retrieved from URL

Earnings and unemployment rates by educational attainment, 2015

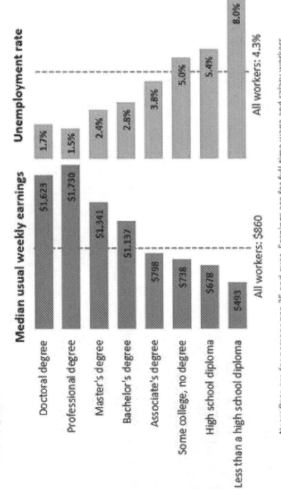

Median usual weekly earnings   **Unemployment rate**

Education	Earnings	Unemployment
Doctoral degree	$1,623	1.7%
Professional degree	$1,730	1.5%
Master's degree	$1,341	2.4%
Bachelor's degree	$1,137	2.8%
Associate's degree	$798	3.8%
Some college, no degree	$738	5.0%
High school diploma	$678	5.4%
Less than a high school diploma	$493	8.0%

All workers: $860   All workers: 4.3%

Note: Data are for persons age 25 and over. Earnings are for full-time wage and salary workers.
Source: U.S. Bureau of Labor Statistics, Current Population Survey

Bureau of Labor Statistics, (2015) *Employment Projections*. Retrieved from URL

Quotes
from three
HBCU Alumnae

"

I attended an HBCU, because of my friends. We chose the schools because of their Christian principles. We also looked at the teacher/student ratio. Smaller classes meant more attention to students and their needs. The most important reason was job placement. The friendships I made in college are still my friends today. Going to an HBCU was one of my best decisions.

Edward Waters and FAMU

Anna J. Westmore

" Based on my experience as an HBCU alumni, I would recommend any student to attend an HBCU. Attending an HBCU and learning from an African Centered Perspective would allow students to love who they are, give them a since of self and pride to conquer the many challenges and barriers they may face. Attending an HBCU would allow students the gateway to become future innovators, inventors, and scholars. "

Clark Atlanta University

Dr. Daphne Cooper

"

I would recommend that students attend an HBCU because, I had a great learning experience. And the pride gained while attending is unforgettable. I established great relationships with many others that possess the same cultural and moral values as I do. These relationships have helped me with both personal and professional decision making.

"

Alcorn State University and Jackson State University

Arnater Martin Dowers

Notable people who attended HBCUs

EXECUTIVES

John W. Thompson

As a graduate of Florida A&M University, John W. Thompson currently serves as the first black chairman of Microsoft Corporation and is the CEO of Virtual Instruments. Before joining the board at Microsoft, he was the vice president at IBM and the CEO of Symantec Corporation.

Oprah Winfrey

An alum of Tennessee State University, Oprah Winfrey is the chairman and CEO of Harpo Productions and the CEO of Oprah Winfrey Network

Black Enterprise (October 27, 2014), 9 Black Executives who Attended HBCUs. Retrieved from URL

ENTERTAINERS

Taraji P. Henson

Toni Braxton

The Grammy award winner briefly pursued a teaching degree at Bowie State University before leaving to focus on music.

Before becoming an award-winning actress and the matriarch of a highly dysfunctional fictional hip-hop family, Henson briefly attended North Carolina Agricultural and Technical State University, where she studied electrical engineering, before transferring to Howard University, where she graduated with a degree in theater.

Buzz Feed (October 28, 2015) *Some of Entertainments biggest names are HBCU alum.* Retrieved from URL

ATHLETES

Donald Driver

Driver was a seventh-round selection of the Green Bay Packers out of Alcorn State in 1999 and he would go on to have one of the best careers in history. He retired as the Packers' all-time leader in receptions and receiving yards and was also selected to three Pro Bowls during his 14-year career. The capper, no doubt, was being a member of the Packers' Super Bowl XLV championship e most prolific careers in club team.

Michael Strahan

Strahan is a member of the Pro Football Hall of Fame Class of 2014. Strahan was a second-round selection of the New York Giants out of Texas Southern in the 1993 NFL Draft. He quickly became one of the most-feared pass rushers as he twice led the league in sacks. His biggest season came in 2001 when he set the NFL single-season record with 22.5 sacks and won the Associated Press NFL Defensive Player of the Year Award. Strahan also went out on top as the Giants bested the New England Patriots in Super Bowl XLII.

NFL (February 10,2014), NFL players from Historically Black Colleges. Retrieved form URl

POLITICIANS

Rev. Jesse Jackson

Rev. Jackson's journey to a life involving activism and politics started during his time at popular HBCU, North Carolina A&T State University. Jackson participated in marches with the late Dr. Martin Luther King Jr. and created Operation PUSH and the Rainbow Coalition, organizations that fought for the betterment of lower class African-Americans and beyonc. In 1983, he became the second African-American to run for president. Today, Jackson continues to advocate for African-Americans who have faced prejudice and racism at the hands of law enforcement

Tanya Walton Pratt

Judge Pratt attended Spelman College and obtained her law degree from Howard University. After working for an associate attorney for several years, she was nominated by President Obama to the United States District Court for the Southern District of Indiana. Winning 95-0, she was elected Indiana's first African-American federal judge.

News One (December 2015), Sky's The Limit: Here Are 9 Black Politicians who went To HBCUs. Retrieved from URL

ENGINEERS

LONNIE JOHNSON

Johnson holds a B.S. degree in Mechanical Engineering, an M.S. degree in Nuclear Engineering, and an honorary Ph.D. in Science from Tuskegee University. Upon graduation, he worked as a research engineer at Oak Ridge National Laboratory's. In 1989, Johnson formed his own engineering firm and licensed his most famous invention, the Super Soaker® water gun, to Laramie Corporation. Two years later, the Super Soaker®, generated over $200 million in retail sales, and became the number one selling toy in America. Currently, Lonnie Johnson holds over 80 patents, with over 20 more pending, and is the author of several publications on spacecraft power systems

Patricia Bath

Doctor Patricia Bath, an ophthalmologist from New York, was living in Los Angeles when she received her first patent, becoming the first African American female doctor to patent a medical invention. The probe patented in 1988, was designed to use the power of a laser to quickly and painlessly vaporize cataracts from patients' eyes, replacing the more common method of using a grinding, drill-like device to remove the afflictions. With another invention, Bath was able to restore sight to people who had been blind for over 30 years. Patricia Bath graduated from the Howard University School of Medicine in 1968 and completed specialty training in ophthalmology and corneal transplant at both New York University and Columbia University.

"Planting the Seeds" Program Activities

Presented by
Carol Hedgepeth

Planting the Seeds

i. Knowledge

A. (September 2016) Orientation for parents and students about the "Planting the Seeds" program.

   a. Informative student packets will be given.
   b. Informative parent packets will be given.

B. (October 2016) Students will be given an overview of HBCU's.

C. (November 2016) Students will provided Long and Short term Goal Setting.

D. (January 2016) Students will began Action Planning for selected colleges.

Planting the Seeds

E. (February 2016) Students will list what and who inspires them.

F. (March – May 2016) Students will participate in STEM workshops activities.

G. (June 2016) Students will review program experiences and attend career fair.

Planting the Seeds

II. Inspiration

A. Students will utilize information provided to become committed to attending an HBCU reflective of career of choice.

B. Student will reach out to selected HBCU's for admission guidelines and resources.

C. Students will develop pride in the purpose and intent of becoming an HBCU alumni.

Planting the Seeds

III. Goal Setting

    A. Identify 4 potential colleges student will consider attending.

    B. Establish a grade point average focus.

    C. Complete 3 information items required for college applications.

IV. Action Steps

A. Maintain a good grade point average.

B. Attend academic enrichment programs/tutorials.

C. Prepare for the ACT & SAT.
   1. Study guides
   2. Online quizzes
   3. Study buddies

D. Prepare a college application essay.

Planting the Seeds

Program Partner:

College Reach Out Program (CROP)

at

Indian River State College

Dr. Danny Hoey

Administrative Director of Minority Affairs

COLLEGE REACH OUT PROGRAM

INDIAN RIVER STATE COLLEGE

INDIAN RIVER STATE COLLEGE is a public, comprehensive college, ranked as one of the best in the nation for its commitment to student success. The College is a national Top Ten Finalist for the prestigious Aspen Prize and ranked as the 9th top public regional college in the South by U.S. News and World Report. Over 30,000 people enroll in IRSC courses each year, attracted by its quality, convenience and affordable tuition. IRSC was designated as the 4th Most Affordable College in the country by the U.S. Department of Education two years in a row, and IRSC students benefit from many scholarship and financial aid opportunities.

Every aspect of IRSC is focused on helping students succeed with small classes, an array of student support services, convenient campuses, and online courses. IRSC has been selected as an Achieving the Dream™ college and recognized for its support of students from enrollment to employment.

IRSC offers over 150 programs, including Bachelor's degrees, Associate in Arts degrees for continuing education at IRSC or a university, Associate in Science degrees for in-demand careers after two years of training, Short-term certificate programs and Quick Job Training.

www.IRSC.edu or 1.866.792.4772

Fort Pierce • Okeechobee
St. Lucie West • Stuart
Vero Beach

Here's How to Apply

Contact your school guidance counselor to connect with the College Reach Out representative at your school for an application.

You may also contact the IRSC Minority Affairs Office at the Main Campus in Fort Pierce for an application packet.

Complete the application and submit it to the Minority Affairs Office.

If you meet the eligibility requirements for the College Reach Out program, you will be invited to interview with the Project Director and counselor.

Parent Association

Parents of College Reach Out students are encouraged to become involved in the academic pursuits of their students. The purpose of the parent association is to promote the goals and objectives of the program and to strengthen the harmony between families, students, staff and the community.

For More Information

Indian River State College
Minority Affairs
3209 Virginia Avenue
Fort Pierce, Florida 34981
Building O, Room 101
Office: (772) 462-7862
Fax: (772) 462-7601

College Reach-Out Program
CROP

(Rev. 6/15)

Program Participants

Program Participation Commitment

Mentor: As a mentor, I commit to:

1. Providing participants with sufficient information to make informed and knowledgeable decisions.
2. Be available at time and dates I have agreed upon.
3. Providing the necessary support assistance and advocacy that will best meet the needs of participants.
4. Serve as a role model for the program.

Student: As a participant I commit to:

1. Completing all actions and activities as appropriate requested of me.
2. Pursue finding answers to any and all questions I may have regarding Historically Black Colleges and Universities.
3. Focus on obtaining the needed assistance that will contribute to improvements in my grade point average.
4. Demonstrate support for other students in as many ways as I can.
5. Showing respect and consideration for all those connected with the program as well as others in my environment.

Mentor Signature: _____ Date: _____

Student Signature: _____ Date: _____

Planting The Seeds

Satisfaction Survey

In order to ensure that we are providing you with the information that you find most helpful, we ask that you complete the satisfaction survey questions listed below.

1. Did this event meet your expectations? _____Yes_____ _____No_____

2. Did you receive answers to all of your questions? _____Yes_____ _____No_____

3. What additional information would you like to be provided?

_____

_____

4. How will you use the information you received from this event?

_____

5. What additional resources or assistance do you need?

_____

6. What final comments or suggestions do you have?

_____

_____

Thank you for your feedback.

The Genius Club Pledge

I am a genius. I can accomplish every goal I set for myself. I am determined to be a high achiever. I will work hard. I will have a plan for my life. I will be all that I can be. This, I promise.

FIRST SESSION

Focus: Knowledge

Description:

September will be viewed as the kick-off for the program with workshops held for both parents and students. The workshop for parents will be titled Parent Night. Parents will be provided an Information Packet giving an overview of the various program components. Discussion will occur regarding the role of the mentors and the expectations for students, The Student Participation form will be distributed and discussed. Parent support will be solicited and questions responded to.

The student workshop will consist of an introduction to the program. This overview will include the program content, expected outcomes; and, the expectations for students and mentors. Students will be advised that the group name will be the Genius Club. The Student Participation form and the Genius Club pledge will be provided. Students will be asked to write 3 questions they have regarding the HBCU's, some possible plans and goals they have for themselves. A key question they will be asked to consider is "Where do you see yourself 5 years from now?"

GENIUS CLUB PLEDGE

I am a genius. I can accomplish every goal I set for myself. I am determined to be a high achiever.

I will work hard. I will have a plan for my life. I will be all that I can be. This, I promise.

SECOND SESSION

1. Our goal for today is to provide you with the first stages of knowledge about the "Planting the Seeds" Program.

2. We will be doing the following:

   A. Describing what the program's intent and content will be.
   B. Describing the expectations for both students and mentors.
   C. Sharing information about the program schedule.
   D. Sharing the encouragement pledge and the participation commitment form.
   E. Having students share what their current knowledge base is about HBCU's.
   F. Having students respond to the following questions:

      (1). Do you have a current goal for what you want to accomplish in life?
      (2). Where do you see yourself 5 years from now?
      (3). What are the 5 most important things you are looking for in a college?

3. The reasons why we are providing this information are:

   A. To begin the process of discussing the value and benefit of HBCU's
   B. To ensure that you apply what you learn (knowledge) in your college decision making process.

4. The actions we will be taking to accomplish our goals are:

    A. Discussing the program's content and intent.
    B. Identifying the expectations for student participation.
    C. Distributing the encouragement pledge and discussing the use and importance of the pledge.
    D. Writing a current personal goal.
    E. Developing questions about HBCU's

SECOND ACTIVITY

Focus: Knowledge

Description:

October will begin the monthly meetings held with students. An in depth overview of HBCU's will occur beginning with the 105 schools and what is offered at each school, narrowing the choices to the top ten and the 4 HBCU's in Florida. Reasons for attending an HBCU will also be discussed. Students will be asked to list 5 things they are looking for in a college. This list will be included in the upcoming sessions as well. Students will participate in the Leaf Activity which requires them to select 4 HBCU's that capture their attention based on the information that has been shared. These 4 HBCU's would then become part of the students' potential list of school choices. Students will be expected to identify for each selected HBCU, the reason for selecting it; how the HBCU will benefit them; and any unanswered questions about the HBCU's they may have. Students will also be given the opportunity to identify any academic concerns or assistance needed for any of the courses they are currently enrolled in at their high schools. Mentors will utilize the information to collaborate with CROP representatives to schedule tutoring sessions for students.

COLLEGE INFORMATION FORM

1. The three most important pieces of information I remember from today are:

    _____

    _____

    _____

2. I will use the information I learned today to:

    _____

    _____

    _____

HBCU QUESTIONS

After listening to today's information, I would like to have the following 3 questions answered:

1._____

_____

_____

2._____

_____

_____

3._____

_____

_____

COURSE FOCUS

Name:_____   Date:_____

Course:_____

Course Focus:_____

Assistance needed:_____
(Show the concept or homework assignment)

HOMEWORK ASSIGNMENT

Take a few minutes to answer the following questions:

1. Where do I see myself in 5 years?_____

_____

_____

_____

2. Where do I see myself in 10 years?_____

_____

_____

_____

PHYLLIS M. WILSON, PH.D

PLANTING THE SEED ACTVITY

Title: Leaves From The Tree

Purpose: Have students learn more about specific HBCU's that align with their career goals.

Activities:

1. Students will utilize the career goals they will be seeking in the future and identify 4 HBCU's that align with these goals based on the research they will conduct regarding what is offered at the HBCU's.

2. Students will write the selected schools on the leaves they will be given.

3. Students will create a list of reasons as to why these schools were chosen and why attending either of these schools would be beneficial for them.

4. A "Learn More" list will be developed reflecting the questions that remain for the students and the information needed that will further contribute to their selection of an HBCU. The outreach and information sources who can best answer questions and provide information for the students will be developed.

5. Mentors will assist students as they pursue the answers and information needed. Mentors will also utilize the "Learn More" lists as part of the planning for the college and job fairs that will occur.

THIRD SESSION PLAN

1. Our goal today is to begin exploring the existing HBCU's.

2. We will be doing the following:

   A. Reviewing the list of the HBCU's and their locations.
   B. Selecting five colleges from the list and placing the names on the leaves.
   C. Utilizing the computer to find information about the 5 chosen colleges.
   D. Discussing what has been found in small groups.
   E. Using the 5 things looked for in a college to see which of the ones selected best match what is looked for.
   F. Completing name tags based on the career choice for the future.
   G. Discussing homework assignment of selecting 10 more of the universities to research on the computer.

3. The reasons why we are providing this information are:

   A. To design a process for independently researching information for specifically selected universities.
   B. To continue to build a knowledge base about HBCU's that will contribute to the college selection process.

4. The actions we will be taking to accomplish our goals are:

   A. Discussing the HBCU's that are available and what it means to each student.

B. Identifying the connection between long term plans and the short terms steps that it will take to accomplish them, i.e. maintaining a good grade point average to be better eligible for scholarships.
C. Repeating the encouragement pledge as a means of motivating students to stay focused.
D. Completing tutoring request form.
E. Emphasizing positive student interaction through small group discussions.

THIRD SESSION ACTIVITY

Focus: Goal Setting

Description: Goal Setting will be the focus of this session with students requested to identify their long and short term goals. A full discussion of the definition of goals; how they are formed; the necessity of having goals; how goals affect decisions and actions; and, the format for writing goals will be discussed prior to the goal development. Students will be given the opportunity to complete the defining goal worksheet as the first step in the process. Students will focus on developing their specific goals with an emphasis on college attendance. Discussion will be led as to why those specific goals were selected. The option to openly share the goals with the entire group will be given. The next portion of the goal development process will be the identification of any possible obstacles to achieving the goals; and, the creation of a plan to overcome the obstacles and the timetable for goal achievement. Students will be requested to complete the course assistance form so that tutoring can be made available.

S.M.A.R.T. Goals
Instructions

When it comes to setting goals, a useful acronym to remember is **S.M.A.R.T.**

Specific: A specific goal has a much greater chance of being accomplished than a general goal. To set a specific goal you must answer the six **"W"** questions:

*Who: *What: *Where: *When: *Which: *Why:

Specific means reasons, purpose or benefits of accomplishing the goal.

EXAMPLE: A general goal would be, "I want to lose some weight." A specific goal would be, "I want to lose 10 pounds in 2 months and I will eat properly and exercise at least 3 days a week to accomplish my goal."

Measurable: - Establish criteria for measuring progress toward the attainment of each goal you set.

Describes how each goal will be measured (numeric or descriptive).

When you measure your progress, you stay on track, reach your target dates, and experience the exhilaration of achievement that spurs you on to continued the effort required to reach your goal.

Ask yourself:

- How will I know when the result has been achieved?
- How will I verify the achievement/performance of this goal?

Attainable: - When you identify a goal, write it out and make a plan, you are making an attainable goal. You will see opportunities arise that will help you in accomplishing this goal. You will develop a positive attitude working towards an attainable goal and you will develop traits that will give you the strength to see it through.

Realistic- To be realistic, a goal must represent an objective toward which you are both *willing* and *able* to work. A goal can be both high and realistic; you are the only one who can decide just how high your goal should be. But be sure that every goal represents substantial progress.

In my book there are no Dreams or Goals too grand, but you do have to be realistic. Make sure the goal you have set is something you are willing and capable of doing. When you set a lofty goal and challenging yourself you will find the reward that much better.

Timely - Creates a sense of urgency. Knowing you have to accomplish a task at a certain time makes you accountable. Know what those time lines are. What needs to be done by when. How much needs to be saved by when and take the steps necessary to meet those timelines.

GoalSettingBasics.com

S.M.A.R.T. Goal Setting Worksheet

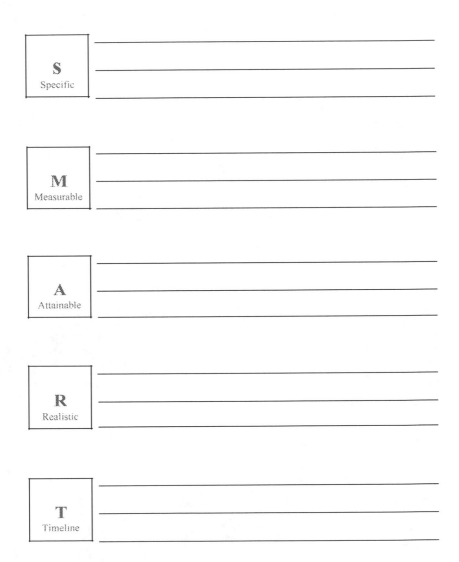

S Specific	_____ _____ _____
M Measurable	_____ _____ _____
A Attainable	_____ _____ _____
R Realistic	_____ _____ _____
T Timeline	_____ _____ _____

Google   definition of goal

All   News   Images   Shopping   Videos   More ...   Search tools

About 615,000,000 results (0.58 seconds)

goal

/gōl/

noun

1. (in football. soccer, rugby, hockey. and some other games) a pair of posts linked by a crossbar and often with a net attached behind it, fanning a space into or over which the ball has to be sent in order to score.

2. the object of a person's ambition or effort; an aim or desired result.
"going to law school has become the most important goal in his life"
synonyms: objective, aim, end, target, design, intention, intent, plan, purpose;
More

Translations, word origin, and more definitions

Goal | Definition of Goal by Merriam-Webster
/www.merriam-webster.com/dictionary/goal • Merriam-Webster ,..
Simple Definition of goal. : something that you are trying to do or achieve.. an area or object into which a ball or puck must be hit, kicked, etc., to score points in various games (such as soccer and hockey)

Goal | Define Goal at Dictionary.com
www.dictionary.com/browse/goal,,,..
The result or achievement toward which effort is directed; aim; end.:..... All thinking towards any goal is a similar instance of the law of combination .... He gave the word and away they sped, this time with the flagship as the goal.

goal definition and synonyms | Macmillan Dictionary
www.macmillandictionary.com/us/../goal • Macmillan English Dictionaries
Define goal and get synonyms. What is goal? goal meaning, pronunciation and more by Macmillan Dictionary.

What is a goal? definition and meaning
www.businessdictionary.com/definitton/goal.html ..
Definition of goal: An observable and measurable end result having one or more objectives to be achieved within a more or less fixed timeframe. For further ...

goal Definition in the Cambridge English Dictionary
dictionary.cambridge.org/.../g ... .- Cambridge Advanced Learner's Dictionary
In some sports, a goal is also the area or netted structure into which a player sends a ball or other object in order to score a point.

Goal - definition of goal by The Free Dictionary
www.thefreedictionary.com/goal ,..
The object toward which an endeavor is directed; an end. See Synonyms at intention. 2. Sports. a. A structure or area into which players endeavor to propel a ...

goal - Dictionary Definition : Vocabulary.com
https://www.vocabulary.com/dictionary/goal •
The goal is the intention of an activity or a plan. In a figurative sense, a goal is the mission of a person or group. A tangible goal could be the net at one end of a ...

goal - definition of goal in English from the Oxford dictionary

MACMILLAN
DICTIONARY

goal- definition and synonyms

NOUN [COUNTABLE] / goal /

Using the thesaurus

Contribute to our Open Dictionary

1   something that you hope to achieve
Our goal is to provide a good standard of medical care.
goal of: *the company's goal of employing as many women as men
within five years*
set/establish a goal: *You should set goals for yourself at the
beginning of each school year.*
achieve/reach/attain a goal: *I haven't yet reached my goal of losing
20 pounds.*

Synonyms and related words

Purposes and intentions: *purpose, role, goal...*

Explore Thesaurus

Related words

goal kick NOUN
goal fine NOUN
own goal NOUN
field goal NOUN
ghost goal NOUN
goal difference NOUN

Collocates: goal

Verbs frequently used with **goal** as the object
· accomplish, achieve, attain, meet, pursue, reach, realize, set

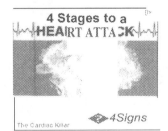

2   an area or structure that a ball must go into or through to score points
in some sports

Synonyms and related words

Sports fields and parts of sports fields: *alley, AstroTurf, baseline...*

Explore Thesaurus

Facebook   Twitter

a.   the action of putting a ball into a goal
score a goal: *Paul scored three goals in the game*
winning goal: *Let's take another look at Italy's fantastic winning
goal.*

Synonyms and related words

Scoring points and goals: *aggregate, ball, assist...*

Explore Thesaurus

b.   the point or points that you score by putting a ball into a goal
At half time, our team was losing three goals to one

Decide What You
Want

Why Is Goal Setting Important?

Learn About Goal
Setting

16 Reasons To Set Smart Goals

getME FREE
2016
Goals
Worksheet
& Plan Your Success Now!

Set Your Smart Goal

Name: _____

_____

Email: _____

_____

Visualize Your Goal

The importance of setting goals

we respect your email privacy

Why is goal setting important?

Take Action

And why must YOU know how to set smart goals?

What are the benefits to you?

⓪neurogym

Stay Motivated

You will experience so many benefits from learning and applying the valuable skill of goal setting the easiest way is to take you through each benefit one by one.

Saturday's Brain-A-thon is a
MUST ATTEND

Here are the top sixteen reasons:-

1) You will move away from the vague 'shoulds' and 'wishes' of your life to a life where you get clear on what you really want and generate the motivation to make it happen.

2) You will learn to always start your thinking by asking yourself what it you really want is.

3) You will have a framework of simple but powerful questions to help you think your goals through thoroughly.

4) You will ask yourself the questions that people who are already successful, your role models for success, ask themselves.

5) You will focus your mind and concentration on what's most important to you.

6) You will end up with your own set of crystal clear goals.

Contribute

7) Having crystal clear goals means you will increase your chances of achieving them

Keep In Touch!

8) You will be able to engage your subconscious to help you achieve your goals, now it knows where you want to go!

Site Info

9) You will get much more out of life.

Recommendations

10) You will learn and do things you have never done before.

11) You will want to develop new skills so that you can achieve what it is you want.

12) You will seek out new information and knowledge to help you achieve your goal.

13) You will broaden and develop who you are as a person:

- Your confidence
- Your motivation
- Your tenacity

14) You will build new beliefs in yourself and start to know just how much more is possible.

15) You will make a difference to the lives of others & perhaps

16) You will make a difference to the lives of your community, country or world as a whole....

Recommended Next Step?

Step 2 of the Smart Goals Success Formula' ™ - ie:

Learn how to set great smart goals!

Return to Goals Mini Course From Why is Goal Setting Important?

243 people like this Sign Up to see what your friends like.

New! Comments

Have your say about what you just read! Leave me a comment in the box below

How High Achievers Set Their Goals: Ebook

What People Are Saying:

"I would have told you I had clear goals, but as a result of the tools I saw they were not nearly as tight as they need to be If I want to quickly build my dreams•.

E. Alana James

Founder - Doctoral Academy

I would highly recommend this process to think through any task that is important to you but may seem unattainable "

Myriam Cronin
Manager
Gateway Incubation Centre University College Cork

"The discipline of working through the steps and key questions in the Smartest Goals process brings exceptional clarity and focus allowing me to achieve much more in a shorter time than I heretofore thought possible.

I would highly recommend this approach to anyone who wishes to achieve their dreams."

Helen O'Dowd
Founder
Virginia Health Foods

"I am delighted with My Smartest Goal!

I was at a bit of a crossroads in my business and I found the entire process most helpful, Insightful, and Inspirational!"

Fiona Foley- Gaffney

1 Comment   Sort by Oldest   **Consultant** Colour Me Beautiful

                                                                                          For More Information Click Here

                    Add a comment...

                    Sarah Moody
                    This has been extremely helpful me, for it has charged me to
                    shoot for my dream and assisted me in finally putting to to
                    paper.
                    Like · Reply · Mar 20, 2015 12:37pm

f Facebook Comments **Plugin**

            Share this page: Facebook   Twitter
            What's this?

                Enjoy this page? Please pay it forward. Here's how :

PLANTING THE SEEDS   I 73

GOAL DEFINING WORKSHEET

o   **What do I want out of life?**_____

_____

o   **What do I enjoy doing?**_____

_____

o   **What am I good at?**_____

_____

o   **What gets me motivated?**_____

_____

o   **Who do I admire and why?**_____

_____

o   **Where do I see myself in 5-10-15 years?**_____

     5_____

     10_____

     15_____

     PHYLLIS M. WILSON, PH.D

COLLEGE INFORMATION FORM

1. The three most important pieces of information I remember from today are:

    _____

    _____

    _____

2. I will use the information I learned today to:

    _____

    _____

    _____

FOURTH SESSION

Focus: Action Planning

Description:

Students will review the goals that have been set; the obstacles they identified; and, the plans for overcoming the obstacles. Conversations will focus on what it will take to achieve each of the selected goals; what will be required of them? What assistance or support will be needed? Who can best help them achieve their goals? And, the level of effort that will be required of them to successfully accomplish the goals? This will also be the month that a College Fair will be held featuring the 4 Florida HBCU's. Students will again be asked to identify any course issues or concerns so that focused tutoring assistance from CROP can be provided.

FOURTH SESSION ACTIVITY

Please give some thought to the following questions as they relate to the achievement of your goals:

1. What will be required of me in order to achieve my goals?

   _____

   _____

   _____

2. Who can best help me achieve my goals?

   _____

   _____

   _____

3. What level of effort will I need to put forth as I work towards my goals? A small amount of effort?_____ A large amount of effort?_____

4. What are the 3 next steps I need to take to begin working on my goals?

   1. _____

   2. _____

   3. _____

COURSE FOCUS

Name:_____   Date:_____

Course:_____

Course Focus:_____

Assistance needed:_____
(Show the concept or homework assignment)

 PHYLLIS M. WILSON, PH.D

FIFTH SESSION

Focus: Inspiration

Description:

The focus of this activity will be to discuss the goals and plans that have been developed, the impact on their future; and, any progress and the level of effort expended for their next steps. Students will be asked to list the people they admire who are most representative of the goals they have set for themselves; why they admire them. Reference to the Goal Defining worksheet will help to respond to these questions. Students will then be asked to list how both their goals and the people they admire have inspirited them as well as having changed the future they now see for themselves. A discussion will be held as to how these factors will contribute to their selection of an HBCU to attend. Students will be given the form "I Am Inspired" to list the ways they have been inspired and to describe the impact on the HBCU decision they made.

INSPIRATIONAL PEOPLE
I HAVE KNOWN

1. Some of the people who have inspired me are:_____

_____

_____

2. The reason each person has inspired me is:_____

_____

_____

3. Because I have been inspired, I plan to:_____

_____

_____

4. My goals have been affected by those who have inspired me in the following ways:_____

_____

_____

 PHYLLIS M. WILSON, PH.D

I AM INSPIRED

The person who inspired me this week is:_____

The reason why I was inspired:_____

The action I will take because I am inspired is:_____

I will use my inspiration to inspire others by:_____

COLLEGE INFORMATION FORM

1. The three most important pieces of information I remember from today are:

_____

_____

_____

2. I will use the information I learned today to:

_____

_____

_____

PHYLLIS M. WILSON, PH.D

COURSE FOCUS

Name:_____   Date:_____

Course:_____

Course Focus:_____

Assistance needed:_____
(Show the concept or homework assignment)

SIXTH SESSION ACTIVITY

Focus: Knowledge

Description:

The focus on STEM (Science, Technology, Engineering, and Math) will begin with information regarding the importance of science; areas covered by science in high school and college. Identifying HBCU's with strong science programs and the potential career possibilities in the science field. Students will be given the opportunity to list 4 science careers that interest them with an assignment asking them to use the internet to explore in more detail the career choices they have chosen. A detailed set of information is requested for students to bring to the next meeting to share with classmates. The presentation students will make to their classmates about their career choices will included describing how this information aligns with the selected HBCU's offerings.

SCIENCE CAREERS I AM INTERESTED IN

1. Name 4 science careers that interest you:_____

    _____

    _____

    _____

2. Explain why you are interested in these particular careers:_____

    _____

    _____

    _____

COLLEGE INFORMATION FORM

1. The three most important pieces of information I remember from today are:

_____

_____

_____

2. I will use the information I learned today to:

_____

_____

_____

HBCU QUESTIONS

After listening to today's information, I would like to have the following 3 questions answered:

1. _____

_____

2. _____

_____

3. _____

_____

I AM INSPIRED

The person who inspired me this week is:_____

The reason why I was inspired:_____

The action I will take because I am inspired is:_____

I will use my inspiration to inspire others by:_____

PHYLLIS M. WILSON, PH.D

EPILOGUE

This curriculum content was developed as a tribute to the many minority students I served as an educator. Many of these students had much in common with me. I grew up on the West side of Chicago surrounded by family on both sides. College was an unknown experience for my family members. A high school diploma was a rare accomplishment, one not held by many of my aunts or uncles. There were few role models for high school completion and none for college attendance. College was a far, far place, unknown and unexperienced.

My sister and I broke the mold with my sister attending junior college on Chicago's West side; and, later attending Southern Illinois University for a short period of time. For me, I decided in the fifth grade that college was some place I wanted to go. I had no idea where college was or where it was located. By the time I was a junior in high school, I had begun to explore where I would attend college. There were no guidance counselors at my high school who had this discussion with an African American female. I was left on my own to discover which college I would attend. No one mentioned Historically Black Colleges and Universities as an option. I had no idea they existed.

My final college choice was determined by a number of factors-the full college tuition paid by the State of Illinois if attendance occurred at any one of the state universities; the fact that my boyfriend would also be attending the college I selected; and, the decision of my sister as well as one of our neighbor's to attend the same university as my boyfriend. I learned about the full tuition from this neighbor whose school guidance counselor had given her this information. She was kind enough to share it with my sister and me. My decision as to which college was based on my limited knowledge; but most of all, by the financial relief provided by the State of Illinois.

Once I became a superintendent of a large minority student population, I made a full commitment to ensure that my students, beginning with kindergarten, would be given as much information as possible about college and the possibilities and rewards college attendance would bring. I wanted my students to be far more astute about envisioning college as a part of their future than I had been. As I met and interacted with a variety of professionals, I heard many conversations about their experiences attending an HBCU. Their pride, their connection to the HBCU; their long term friendships with other attendees made me very envious. I was in no way linked to the universities I had attended in any way close to their experiences.

As luck would have it, when I was nominated to become a member of a national organization, along with two others, the initiative we were assigned to develop and implement was for Historically Black Colleges and Universities. As the initiative was created and developed, there was so much that I learned and absorbed. I became one of the greatest fans and supporters of attendance at HBCUs. It didn't matter which one. There was much to be gained from the experience, not only skills that lead to employment; but, lifelong friendships that extended beyond the college years.

For all of the reasons shared above, it is my wish to further make available to all potential college attendees, a full overview of Historically Black Colleges and Universities and the benefits gained from attending them. This book is my tribute to Historically Black Colleges and Universities. Please take all of the information provided for presentations to students in grades six through nine and share it with as many potential HBCU attendees as possible. Use the information well and wisely. The end result will be students who are successful and who will gain all that they need for the positive future they so deserve.

ABOUT THE AUTHOR AND CONTRIBUTORS

Phyllis M. Wilson is a well educated (B.S. from Southern Illinois University; M.A. from Roosevelt University; and, a PH. D. from The Ohio State University) and fully experienced educator. Her experiences range from a beginning career in the Chicago Public Schools as an Elementary teacher and School Counselor to a wide range of positions in Dayton, Ohio (from a Supervisor of Severe Behavior Handicapped Students, to a Director/ Principal for Special Education); positions in Columbus, Ohio (Supervisor for Curriculum and Program Development for Special Education, Executive Director for Special Education, Assistant Superintendent for Curriculum and Instruction, Interim Superintendent/Chief Academic Officer, Chief Academic Officer, and Deputy Superintendent. The final career position for Dr. Wilson was as the Superintendent for District 86 in Joliet, Illinois.

In addition to her career positions, Dr. Wilson also worked as an Adjunct Professor for Northeastern University and Capella University. She received many awards and recognitions including the De La Salle Award from Lewis University; the Peace Award for Organizational Achievement from the Illinois Center for Violence Prevention; the Athena Award from the Joliet Chamber of Commerce; and Certificates of Recognition from the Illinois House of Representatives and The Ohio House of Representatives. Dr. Wilson's entire career was based on the desire to create the best possible learning environment for students as well as for continuous personal growth and improvement. It is the lessons she has learned and the knowledge she has gained from her experiences that are shared in this book. It is her hope that all who read it will learn and grow so that their impact on children will be all that it should be.

Carol Hedgepeth

Contributor

I Carol Hedgepeth studied fashion design and merchandising at the Fashion Institute of Technology in New York. Eventually I left the design world to pursue a interest in Skin care, attended Capri in New Jersey and became a licensed Esthetician, Aroma therapist skin care formulator from The Florida College of National Health. After working with plastic surgeon and dermatologist for eight years. I then became the owner and founder of Skin Essentials skin care center in Miami Florida for ten years. Where I had the opportunity to work with a wide variety of clientele such as Madonna, The Bob Marley Family, The Miami Heat and Their wives, Cheerleader Singer and Models.

Personal

Married to Dr. Quinton Hedgepeth 2 daughters

Dr. Brittany Hedgepeth graduated from the University of Miami Miller School of Medicine

Dominique Hedgepeth graduated from the University of Florida, Bachelor degree in Animal Science.

In Miami I was a member of The Miami Bridge for Children, The Children Homes Society,

Honey Shine Mentoring Program, Bethel Baptist Church girls Leadership Program

Jack and Jill of America

In Port St Lucie Young Leaders of tomorrow, rendered skin care and wellness workshops.

Member of the Treasure Coast Chapter Links, Incorporated.

*   *   *

Arnater Martin Dowers

Contributor

Arnater Martin Dowers is a Medical Technology instructor who sees education as an important tool to life. She was born in Chicago, Illinois but spent most of her childhood in the Mississippi delta. Arnater currently lives in Port Saint Lucie, Fl with her husband Dante Dowers and son Nigel Dowers.

After graduating high school in Shaw, Mississippi Arnater attended Alcorn State University (HBCU). She later went on to complete her Bachelors of Science degree at the University of Southern Mississippi. Arnater started her professional career at the University of Mississippi Medical Center in Jackson, Mississippi as a Medical Technologist. After working there for a couple of years she was promoted to technical supervisor. And later served as interim chief technologist. While in this role she completed her Master of Public Health Degree at Jackson State University (HBCU). She is currently in pursuit of her Doctoral degree from NOVA Southeastern University. Arnater spent eight years of her professional career as a Medical Technologist working at Cleveland Clinic Martin Health System.

Because Arnater enjoyed training new employees and students in her many roles as a Medical Technologist, she decided to pursue her passion and is now working for Indian River State College as a professor. She has since obtained an additional credential from the Association of College and University Educators and has received a certificate in effective college instruction.

When Arnater is not working she is volunteering throughout her community. She has volunteered at several health fairs and college fairs. Arnater was also feature in several news article related to breast cancer awareness, metabolic syndrome and other critical health issues. She was also interviewed by the local channel 5 news team on the importance of the Medical Technology program at Indian River State College.

Some of her hobbies include most importantly being a Mom, traveling, shopping, dancing, and attending Broadway shows.

Printed in the United States
by Baker & Taylor Publisher Services